THE SIREN IN THE TWELFTH HOUSE

Copyright © Victoria Mbabazi, 2024
All rights reserved

Palimpsest Press
1171 Eastlawn Ave.
Windsor, Ontario. N8S 3J1
www.palimpsestpress.ca

Printed and bound in Canada
Cover layout and typography by Ellie Hastings
Cover Artwork by Isabella Fassler
Edited by Jim Johnstone

Palimpsest Press would like to thank the Canada Council for the Arts and the Ontario Arts Council for their support of our publishing program. We also acknowledge the assistance of the Government of Ontario through the Ontario Book Publishing Tax Credit.

LIBRARY AND ARCHIVES CANADA CATALOGUING IN PUBLICATION

TITLE: The siren in the twelfth house / Victoria Mbabazi.
NAMES: Mbabazi, Victoria, author.
IDENTIFIERS: Canadiana (print) 20240424387
             Canadiana (ebook) 20240424441
ISBN 9781990293795 (SOFTCOVER)
ISBN 9781990293801 (EPUB)
SUBJECTS: LCGFT: Poetry.

CLASSIFICATION: LCC PS8625.B33 S57 2024 | DDC C811/.6—DC23

THE SIREN IN THE TWELFTH HOUSE

VICTORIA MBABAZI

CONTENTS

PART ONE

The Siren in the Twelfth House / 11
Element: Water (Wash) / 12
Cardinal Lovers / 13
Eleventh House Whirlwind / 14
Sister Signs: Pisces And Virgo Write About Blooming / 15
An Assessment of the Tenth House / 17
Ninth House Target Practice / 19
Sister Signs: Aquarius And Leo Write A Play At The Movies / 20
Element: Fire (Leave Me On Fire Or Not At All) / 22
Succumb in the Eighth House / 23
Seventh House Love Story / 25
Sister Signs: Capricorn Tells Cancer The Wolf Loves The Moon / 26
Fixed Lovers / 28
Cheese Platter for the Sixth House / 29
Game Night at the Fifth House / 30
Sister Signs: Sagittarius Goes To Gemini For Confession / 31
Element: Earth (Waltzing Off A Cliff) / 33
The Anatomy of the Fourth House / 34
The Third House is a Padded Room / 35
Sister Signs: Scorpio And Taurus Should Get Divorced / 37
Ingest The Second House / 38
Burn The First House Down / 39
Sister Signs: Libra Puts Aries On Trial / 40
Element: Air (Discard At Daybreak) / 43
Mutable Lovers / 44

PART TWO

Statements in the First House / 47
South Node / 49
Element: Air (The Siren Is Air Surfing) / 50
The Acquisition of the Second House / 52
Synastry: Opposition (Their Moon Is In Aries) / 53
Third House Mind Palace / 54
Fourth House Inventory / 56
Synastry: Square (To You For Me) / 57
Element: Earth (This Siren Is Sprinting) / 59
Fifth House Theatre / 61
Propagating The Sixth House / 63
Synastry: Inconjunct (The Sun Was In Pisces) / 64
Midheaven / 66
Slow Dance in the Seventh House / 71
Eighth House Miracle / 72
Synastry: Trine (To Me For You) / 73
Element: Fire (That Siren Is Setting Fires) / 74
Ninth House Stellium / 75
    1. Siren Migration
    2. Rodeo Clowns
    3. A New Space
Deliverance From the Tenth House / 78
Synastry: Sextile (The Island Rose In Cancer) / 80
The Basement in the Eleventh House / 81
Inventing the Twelfth House / 83
Element: Water (These Sirens Are Swimming) / 85
Synastry: Conjunct (Sun Song) / 87
North Node / 88

Acknowledgements / 89
About the Author / 91

We are in the age of Aquarius, this age signifies an era that will bring harmony to the world.
We are not free until we are all free.
Free Congo. Free Sudan. Free Palestine.

PART ONE

and behold, a great wind came from across the wilderness and struck the corners of the house [...] and I alone have escaped to tell you.
– Job 1:19

THE SIREN IN THE TWELFTH HOUSE

truthfully I can only tell you what's missing
if love is oxygen it's done nothing but die here
it's yet to acclimate to my home's density
but truth can exist without intimacy
I'll try it out I won't lie if you can guess

what I'm feeling in a round of charades
or hangman the rope tied around my neck
and I know I shouldn't make this a game
but how else are you supposed to know
I'm someone worth losing I've decided

on Russian roulette you go first new rules
aim straight all the ammunition boomerangs
and when you shoot hope that bullet
doesn't come back to haunt you I'm sorry
I know it's hard to have fun while drowning

but it's not my fault you decided to follow a siren
into the ocean I'm sorry—when you pulled
the trigger the impact muffled
no one heard the gun go off
fire is timid underwater but I know you felt it

I know you're going to tell me it didn't hurt
you're spilling out misery tinting the water red
it's my turn but we're out of bullets
and even if we weren't I can't see
clearly your heart keeps getting between us

ELEMENT: WATER
The Siren imagines an ending during a storm

WASH

the sky is fractured by
the approaching hurricane

it paints the air a soft blue
hardened by thundering
harsh and apocalyptic

the room wrestling with floating
pages the aroma of coffee
burning the singing knives
hitting near empty plates

declarations turning into
haunting observations they make
their way up our throats tell me
you love me I thought endings

foreshadowed you don't have to
die here you don't mind you
stand up resigned

I'm the only one who'll
survive this hurricane

the cracked windows

still hoping you'll tell me
you love me

CARDINAL LOVERS
Former lovers are reduced to constellations, they'll die far from us

ARIES

love is gasoline
fire is unavoidable
I resent when I became
an ocean do not ruin us
with the truth do not
neglect to set us on fire

                                    CANCER

                I can only tell you what's missing
                    tell me you love me ignore
                        warning signs turbulence
              ignore my heart beating through
                          the heels of my feet
                          try instead run to me

LIBRA

you didn't want to hunt for me
our years compressed to days
love is afterbirth life is more
than you happening to me
there is a hole forming
in the drywall you always meant to leave

                                CAPRICORN

                      this love is a reckoning
                    I am evident in those
                    who go through me
                if an apple dies as I fall
          into an ocean I don't want to know

ELEVENTH HOUSE WHIRLWIND

descartes couldn't have made better use of my time all the dykes I know discovered they were dykes in isolation all the dykes I know discovered they were they in isolation I think therefore the gayer I become

with no one looking I had to see myself without influence my body belongs to me my mind and soul are aligning your love is an airborne virus

and all my panicked breaths are a little too deep this union sets and mutates in the west and the only cure is a very focused comet I got no worries I am divinely protected all the dykes I know became astrologers in isolation

they told me the sky is falling and that you're ready for reconciliation I am at the finish line past the cusp of a love story

and ending I've gone stargazing the water bearer sent our cards to the wind you will not be another tower moment I am mid air thrown up in the wreckage of our home darling I've fallen in love

with the tornado that blew it to pieces my death could mean paradise I can almost see it the sky bluer than I've known it the grass as green as green can be I'll ignore warnings of turbulence

you see we've without a doubt reached your ending and it better hurt when daylight tears through skin

SISTER SIGNS
If love can't be a house it will be a garden

PISCES AND VIRGO WRITE ABOUT BLOOMING

Dear Pisces,

We are losing the pothos. I'm not sure how it happened. I've been told they are hard to kill—they call them devil's Ivy. Surely, you must have a cure. Tell me something: is it the dirt it is grown on? I've worked hard to make it fertile. I've worked hard, I've written to you three times. Are your letters losing ink underwater? Please, tell me why you would start a garden with me without intent to maintain it? I thought you wanted proof that life is more than what happens to us. You watched the flowers bloom and I showed you "God as shrubbery." That's what you said, a silly sentiment. Though I was happy you were enchanted. Please say something. *Tell me love is like grass or whatever else is plentiful. I know you believe even the weeds are gorgeous. Yet, we are losing the pothos, its golden leaves yellowing. In a way that indicates decay. Everything else is fine. I just loved those the most—we rooted them together—where have you been? Have your letters drowned underwater? I've written to you with waterproof paper, waterproof ink. By this I mean, you must be ignoring me. I don't know if I deserve it. I hope to hear from you soon.*

Concerned,

Virgo

My dearest Virgo,

I'm sorry my love but I have found myself preoccupied. I'm on the hunt to kill all that is wrong with me. Though more relatedly, I was overwatering our garden. When I realized I was the problem I took a step back. I took in what you said about weeds and remembered that although the pothos is gorgeous it is an invasive plant. It was killing every other plant in our garden. I've been the one destroying the devil's ivy, my darling. We must let it die. I predict tomorrow the roses will bloom again—you know they haven't flowered in some time. I'll be over tomorrow a little before sunset. We can watch the sky blossom into pink. I want to have dinner with you. I'll tell you I'm sorry...I'll tell you I love you. Whether or not you forgive me, the pothos will die and the garden will continue to live.

Love
Pisces

Pisces,

I'll make stew.

<u>*Deeply annoyed,*</u>

Virgo

My dearest Virgo,

I love stew.

Full of love,

Pisces

AN ASSESSMENT OF THE TENTH HOUSE

Psychiatric Consultation:

Pisces, a young siren in their twenties, came in with their heart beating through the heels of their feet.

Reason For Referral:

Sleepless nights or nights where dreams seep into reality. There was a day they came home and it was raining in their living room. Very strange they said—the way the rain never touched the carpet. They thought maybe it would cleanse the house. They said they should've soaped the floors so the downpour could have washed them more thoroughly.

History Of Presenting Illness:

Some days the siren stares at walls waiting for them to crack and cave in. They asked if I'd ever done that. I said the walls aren't damaged in this house. They said Capricorn would love that. Capricorn is their mother. I told them she helped build the tenth house. They said that explained the home's coldness. I asked them to explain further, and they said Virgo tried to kill himself months after they were born. Virgo is their father. They said their mother told him that maybe if he waited he would've seen that life would end him slowly, that he could cave with it. They said she almost promised him.

Medical History:

Pisces has visited the doctor over ten times in two months. They're experiencing pain in various parts of their body. Said they're in the process of rebuilding houses. Said every house they enter destroys itself. Said a tidal wave put their home underwater. There are bruises all over their body. I asked how they got them. They said the damage was from the tornado that hit the eleventh house. They said the houses seemed determined to fall apart. I told Pisces a house couldn't be responsible. They told me they're afraid they're responsible for the homes' undoing.

Social and Developmental History:

The siren was an insecure and lonely child. They hate everything about themself from the scar on their knee to the way they apologize any time someone looks them in the eyes. They never learned how to stop apologizing. They said as the keeper of the twelfth house they aren't used to being more than a shadow in a room and now it's like they can't escape their skin. They don't remember when they became a living thing. They said they've always felt too much. A house dies every time they fall in or out of love. I asked if a house fell when they were in and out or in or out of love. They said they can't tell the difference. It doesn't matter anyway. If they were in love this house would collapse.

Mental Status Examination:

They said *I'm good* and asked to leave. I asked them to stay a little longer. They said they were thankful and repeated that they were okay. They said it staring at the floor. They looked up and pointed to the corner of my office. There was a hole forming in the drywall. They said I should check the pipes, it could just be water damage. They said it was lucky we caught it on time. The siren smiled and promised I'd be fine.

NINTH HOUSE TARGET PRACTICE

If the carpet is red you can't see
the blood on the floor take that
advice for the couch the table the walls
it'll be a new space let it be loud unafraid
of its darkness you're impatient but I miss
tension if it is butter set it out let it melt over
the counter I like stray arrows elephants
roaming around our living room

if I get shot we'll dye the curtains red
is passion that's what you wanted love
as renewal love is afterbirth it is bloody
dear god if you didn't want to hunt for me
you should've came with more answers
than questions I'm not inquisitive I'm not
interested in knowing I love cliff hanging
I want undertones between lines edging prey

running from our bedroom and I'm sorry
you should've shredded the lease you
should've read the fine print this love
is a reckoning its death will be quick
unsatisfying you were always a pierced heart
my love was always an arrow and I'd rather
the house be covered in blood than bleach
or empty apologies I'd rather fight

around it than about it
let's aim for moving targets bystanders
dying in our kitchen please don't tell
me you're sorry because I know
what will happen if we cut
the tension I don't want to be the one
left bleeding out on the table

SISTER SIGNS
If Love is not a house let it be a performance

AQUARIUS AND LEO WRITE A PLAY AT THE MOVIES

"I think that our love is passionate—until I watch you do anything else." — Leo, *first act, opening scene, opening line*

"When I take her to the movies I want our love to feel like a montage. Brief, eclectic. I want to never be bored."
—Aquarius, *second act, scene two, lines 1-5*

"I see myself as a great actress but I have no idea who you're performing for. Tonight's show is *Inception* over *Napoleon Dynamite*. I pretend I haven't seen it. You like that best. You want to tell me about yourself without telling me."—Leo, *third act, closing scene, lines one-six*

"I want to believe my friends when they say that we look happy together, but I can't tell you anything. Everything gets stuck in my throat. I want you to know me. When you eat with your eyes you can't choke on anything."
—Aquarius, *fourth act, opening scene, lines 4-9*

"All I know is that you may or may not be
funny. That you may or may not love llamas.
That you like a gradient that is pale piercing
and sunburnt. I am ruled by the sun so I guess
that means you love me as I am. I can't love
the shadow of you and you won't lean in out of the dark."
— Leo, *fourth act, closing scene, lines 10-14*

"I'm afraid I'll be left as smoke
if you walk away. I'm afraid
I'll never tell you. You'll leave me choking."
—Aquarius, *act one, opening scene, lines 1-3*

"When you lost me the only shock
was your disappointment."
— Leo, *closing act, closing scene, closing line*

ELEMENT: FIRE
The Siren imagines they end in arson

LEAVE ME ON FIRE OR NOT AT ALL

douse our house in gasoline trash all the things I gave you the sweaters the flowers the socks with the receipts

steal the silverware that mug with the first letter of my name on it steal my jewellery my scarf my only good pair of pants thanks for the inconvenience block me on facebook block me on twitter block me on instagram dump the friends we shared

tell your mom you don't know me anymore delete our pictures block my number vague me on your snapchat story—block me on snapchat—but you forget to leave me

forget the dent in my pillow your perfume still permeates the sweaters the stuffed toy you bought me is still on the floor in my room the room you wouldn't let me sleep in until I was done being mad at you

I said sleep next to me I said let's never leave each other angry you said let's never leave each other

you kept your promise you're haunting I can't scrub you off I need an exorcism you leave hair in the shower clog the drain I thought you'd drown me

removing the carpet won't erase your steps you steal the lighters the matches how dare you douse our house in gasoline and neglect to set it on fire

SUCCUMB IN THE EIGHTH HOUSE

my heart is on the other side of this door
we have eight minutes take off all
your clothes this will not be my undoing
flight is possible on the other side
you can float

        with me love is gravity
        I don't want to be tethered
        heaven is fog on the water
        and if this organ has to be light
        as a feather I'll go missing
        sans choir I can already feel

my disappearance you offer neck kisses
softness I want to be drained fucking
you is just to say it happened you're
collateral my life is evident in those
who go through me my body disagrees
it won't let you go

        through me the house
        begins to shake I neglected
        to tell you my heart's a bomb
        I was trying to save you
        but it beats to implode
        I didn't mean to love you

like this how could anyone love me
like this love is grounding
it's not safe to feel deeper than this
I kept one promise I float up the ceiling
is cloud nine I've already hit the self
destruct

button don't bother with
crossed wires just close
your eyes you won't see me
coming—I'm sorry I didn't
warn you I always meant
to leave this undone

SEVENTH HOUSE LOVE STORY

I do not mourn the days we spent together I mourn
the depth they promised I mourn
the dreamscape I built the disillusioned castle on top
of the grassy hill the way the sunset framed
it in glass took only one arrow to shoot and break
through it how beautiful it was our first
kiss the matt at the front door our first
I love you said twenty different ways
decorating the halls the kitchens the
first to third floor that time in that meadow that
time in Paris that time at the edge of the world
I only fell off once but came back to life
just to say it for the first and final time
in our home the one with the baskets
of roses hanging from the ceiling with hardwood floors
and a direct view failing to reach impact
I watched it all collapse the postcard landscape folding
in on itself the rooms of false memory disappearing
as our time comes to a close our final days
on the fourth floor we're in the rocking chairs on our porch
facing our ending the way we died
as the sky fell into the night the weight of our years
to be together compressed to months compressed to days
to hours I wish we'd survived

SISTER SIGNS
If love can't be a house it should reinvent itself

CAPRICORN TELLS CANCER THE WOLF LOVES THE MOON

Cancer: I just need more than whatever love language you think this is I just don't believe you—

Capricorn: What more do I have to say—

Cancer: It's not enough to say or to do or to move you walk around it I just I can't tell you I love you if when you show me it's like watching someone drown explaining how the car door is open from the outside in—

Capricorn: I love you it wasn't hard to say I say it everyday what else do you want me to be—

Cancer: I want your love to be a current to breathe underwater I want you to just try to love me like I'm on life support—

Capricorn: Cancer darling you must see the irony—

Cancer: I'm a cardinal sign I am not above violence thank you—

Capricorn: I'm sorry—

Cancer: I need more than a statement I want walls falling tell me about me tell me how you love me I feel like you don't know me—

Capricorn: I love you the way the wolf loves the moon I wait for you I don't run because no matter where I am you're all I see—

Cancer: That's not good enough—

Capricorn: This whole thing is boring you know you're coming home with me tonight—

Cancer: I am the moon—

Capricorn: And you are all I see—

Cancer: You're not a wolf—

Capricorn: I don't need to call to you you're already home to me—

Cancer: Love me like you're renovating like you can always see me as something new—

Capricorn: You can't be serious—

Cancer: Please I want to know that we are always worth fixing—

Capricorn: What is there to fix—

Cancer: Something eventually—

Capricorn: I guess I can love you like we could use new kitchen countertops—

Cancer: Thank you that's all I ask

FIXED LOVERS
Former lovers are reduced to constellations, they die far from us

TAURUS

love is grounding
my heart is on the other side
of this door I'll go missing
sans choir stop stand over
there you didn't warn me
I could die in the oven

                                            LEO

                I don't want to be left bleeding out
                on the table I am good at knowing
                        the mood who will survive
                love is oxygen and it's done nothing
                                but die here

SCORPIO

I think I know you you're not a wolf
I can't love the shadow of you lean
out of the dark watch the sky blossom
to pink you are not a siren you are not
meant to survive this

                                    AQUARIUS

              what keeps my mother alive our
          house is paradise I am not bottomless
                    full of limitations delusion
                          occupies our house
          I'd do anything to be part of your day

CHEESE PLATTER FOR THE SIXTH HOUSE

I can't live without the soft cheese I get at this grocery store if I don't have the cheese what else am I supposed to pair the crackers and meats with and don't say a different cheese I've been there I've tried them all and this is the first time I've actually craved real cheese perfect cheese not

cheese whiz or the cardboard with sodium that comes in those little plastic wrappers that you use to make sandwiches but this cheese is the perfect amount of soft and its herbal too and spreadable it's not too tangy or too bitter it doesn't hurt my stomach like the other cheeses did and so what if in the long run it kills me what's the point

of living if you don't have all the parts that make you happy and don't say there will be other parts because I've seen them the bread always goes stale after a day I mean I guess it wouldn't if I tied the bag but who has the time and I tried loving milk but by the time I get to it it's rotten or about to be and I guess it wouldn't be about to be or already rotten if I just drank it but I don't want to I want the soft cheese I've had every week

for the past six months the first thing to make me happy since you discontinued the last thing to make me happy so don't tell me I can't have this anymore I come here because it is the only place I can get it don't say it's gone because it wasn't healthy please stop saying I'll get used to it if you don't give it to me I'll go somewhere else I'm so afraid that if I'm elsewhere

I'll find another version and that I won't even be able to pretend to enjoy it that maybe I love this toxic waste soft cheese because I can feel my heart failing every time I eat it so how about this how about you give me one last moment with it I know you have one pack in the back so just one final moment before it's over because it's no good for me and then how about then you let it end me

GAME NIGHT AT THE FIFTH HOUSE

Do you want me
to put poison in the wine I'm drinking
or in the beer you'll drink later?
Are you still mad at me?
If an Apple dies as a tree
falls into an ocean
are you still staying the night?
Do you want to leave me?

I love party games
Mafia is my favourite
You are good at killing
loving is better
familiar and fatal

I am good at knowing
the mood of a door
when it closes
If the tap is crying
when it doesn't shut
all the way off I am good

at engulfing my space
the couch is capable of breathing
and it keeps breaking its legs
I can be good I promise
I am great at becoming
whatever you want me to be
Give me a second give me time

Let me show you I promise
I can walk back into that burning Target
and remember all the things
you wanted from the store

SISTER SIGNS
If love can't be a house it can be a series of questions

SAGITTARIUS GOES TO GEMINI FOR CONFESSION

[1] Father Sagittarius entered the holy temple to meet Father Gemini in confession. A burden deep in his heart. Dear father, Sagittarius said. [2] Gemini did not know what Sagittarius was carrying. He came into the holy house with levity. Yes daddy, Gemini said.

[3] Sagittarius was not amused. He was not interested in games. That's only funny in private, he said, hoping it would indicate that he was coming to the priest for peace of mind. [4] We are in private, Gemini said. Gemini considered their holy house a safe space.

[5] No we are not, Sagittarius said. It was important to him that his brother knew God was watching over them. God is always watching, Gemini said. He knew very well. He was not a stupid man. I have specifically called upon his presence, Sagittarius said.

Not everything has to be a joke, the centaur reminded him. [6] It is more fun when it is, Gemini reminded back. Please, Sagittarius begged, I brought you to confession as a witness. I am your witness, Gemini said. We can talk anywhere.

[7] I want a witness who will judge me, Sagittarius said. You are too jovial to do so. I need you here to feel safe. God is everywhere, Gemini reminded him. Shut up, Sagittarius demanded him. I want to be held accountable.

[8] I am the reason the siren is destroying the houses, the centaur admitted. I don't think you can blame yourself for that, Gemini said. The priest was of two minds. He believed in confession and he believed in honesty but he valued nuance. They've been hurt the same way by many people, Gemini said.

[9] I know but I think I started the pattern, Sagittarius said. The centaur felt as though his heart was bleeding all over the floor. Coming to terms with what happened felt like a game of darts where he was the target. This confession is useless, Gemini said. Father, Sagittarius responded. Gemini shook his head and put his finger over Sagittarius's mouth. He did not want him to speak.

[10] You think they'd learn after some time that you can't save a person into loving you. Love may be service but no one stays on the arc that saved them. Gemini held his brother's hand. I treated their love like I was a shark, Sagittarius said. [11] By that he meant he loved them through drowning and when he stopped swimming he thought their love would die too.

Stillness is not a death, Gemini declared. The house is still alive underwater. Sagittarius shook his head. But he wanted his brother to understand.

It sank because of me, Sagittarius confessed. [12] When it fell I saw ruins. What else were you supposed to see? Gemini asked. You are not a siren. You weren't meant to survive it.

[13] They drowned it on purpose. They seemed surprised, Sagittarius pointed out. They did it for a purpose, Gemini stated. I could've been kinder. Sagittarius insisted. Gemini squeezed Sagittarius's hand. If confessions are [14] for what ifs, maybe we should stop doing them, Gemini decided. What should we do instead?

Sagittarius asked his brother. You know that it's over, Gemini said. The house is alive and you are in this holy one. Yes, Sagittarius agreed. [15] If they forgive you, if they don't forgive you. You'll never know, Gemini told him. You can't breathe under water.

ELEMENT: EARTH
The siren imagine they end with a concussion

WALTZING OFF A CLIFF

You are very good at dancing I love a good ballad take me by the hand let us dance I am better than you at it

but this is quite the performance gorgeous wow you're sexy damn you're funny too romantic aren't you a sad clown you're quite the actor it's exhausting to always be bitter over your love interests

even if they're just understudies to your mirror you are the love of your life every woman is a casualty they don't believe in their death until their burial you're an earthquake a sudden devastation and I know

your love is not bottomless you are full of limitations—you didn't tell me my head would open as it hit the pavement and that yours is made of rocks

THE ANATOMY OF THE FOURTH HOUSE

I don't want to know
what keeps my mother alive
when she holds me
she is holding her own
face our house is kinetic
it's on its way to collapse

there are other forbidden
fruits and now I know too much
Eve's sons are demons
and she loves them too
I'm sorry I ruined us didn't I

we can't live if I know
I'm dying she said
it can't be forgiven
it's too bad it's happened
now I know the trick
to immortality

our home can be reconstructed
built anew with ribs
knowing I want to die
in your image I do not
know how go screaming
collapse with the house

THE THIRD HOUSE IS A PADDED ROOM

Every time my sister relapses I want a drink I want several
and I'll have them too I want to be just like you withered and
drowning you look great in crop tops and too bright lighting
and when I sent you

to the ward it didn't cost me nothing and I'd do it again and I'll
take another shot to lie better alcohol is a performance enhanc-
ing drug I will be the most vibrant version of the ghost I'm
becoming

I don't want to be nice anymore I'm not a tender poet all the
soft spots are bruises they hurt to touch I was raised on 2000s
sitcoms I'd rather be ironic in my devastation if my life is a
narrative

it means there's a resolution if my life is a movie it means there's
an hour before it starts to make sense press the rewind button
we used to like each other I'd tell you everything I miss you

what version of yourself are you afraid of losing I'm looking
in the mirror and there is nobody there I'm the vampire I was
afraid of loving I'm looking at myself and I'm filling up too
much space after your first love

died you spent three months watering dying plants in the
hopes to save them I forgot how you love I forget when you
love you are nursing when my sister is sober she is cooking for
me I've been starving a long time we are lost

to each other the version I'm afraid of losing is the one you call
yours I was meant to keep you as mythology the rope was tied
around our feet you cut the cord you never learned to float but
I am going to save you I fear nothing

I'll keep fighting for you we belong to each other we are of each other it for each other I need to stop lying—

Delusion occupies the third house

I'm not fighting

when you drowned I ran

SISTER SIGNS
If love can't be a house it should end

SCORPIO AND TAURUS SHOULD GET DIVORCED

> *Every night before Taurus goes to bed*
> *she makes a list of all the pieces Scorpio*
> *cut up of her just to lay next to her*

Curling up under you/I wait for you to die/count all your breaths before I fall asleep/keep thinking about the first day we met/your eyes were every time of day occurring at once/there's a magic to a man who embodies the sky/I've always felt so rooted to the earth/at the right angle trees look like veins/but even the largest trees can never truly bleed into the sky

> *Every morning when Scorpio wakes up he makes*
> *a chart of all the times he thought to leave*
> *wonders if Taurus noticed the packed bag in the closet*

I wanted to be a carpenter/I had no dreams of starting a religion/I'd never read one verse in any holy book/all I remember is that I wanted to create things/tables and chairs maybe even some white picket fences/but I was afraid of cuts from sharp edges/I don't do well with bleeding/when I look at you now I feel every splinter/you were everything I asked for from love/I didn't know I wouldn't be able to love you/but the deepest splinters bleed out/I am unable to pull

> *Everyday the charts and lists get thinner*
> *as our time together thickens*
> *I want to believe we need this but we don't we don't*
> *really*

INGEST THE SECOND HOUSE

oh brother it's just as you promised

the walls are gingerbread gates lifesavers the gummy kind

if I wreck my teeth it'll feel sweet before cracking the witch of the house

is famished she wants me for dinner and I want to get ate but right now

my appetite is bigger she's a stone witch a master of endurance

she'd rather have me seasoned and sauced on the table

I know her strength taught her patience her skin is softness our kisses are

appetizers she likes my kinks she says: "love I'll watch you binge the house down"

the pipes are filled with wine the desserts are running with poison I'm happy

I'll be full for her and perfect for dinner

you said I belonged to you that you knew

I was lust at first sight you said yearning is everlasting especially when it's stolen

I was not worried about my aching teeth your lips still tasted like sweetness

you lit a candle chocolate taste better melting I was not worried about the wine

I wanted to be blacked out you wrapped me in a soft blanket your lips pressed

against my neck wind blowing through the window I tore

through I was so full I fell asleep oh brother you never

warned me I could die in the oven

BURN THE FIRST HOUSE DOWN

if I really love you the poem
will run before it conquers
well fuck that I'm sick

I'm not taking
shelter if our love is gasoline
i'll put it to use look

what I've done I believe
in warmth as creation
our house comes burning

down I'm over reminiscing
I can't keep dreaming of fire
I've started manifesting

I've set it all in flames
I've found the match stomped
on the back of my foot

I can't love anybody
with our foundation still
intact I'm over

returning to a home
that's determined to crumble
the soil has become

radioactive the vultures
have started to unionize
i'm over this

tradition this love
was never worth rebuilding
this time I love me

SISTER SIGNS
If love can't be a house it will be an argument

LIBRA PUTS ARIES ON TRIAL

(*Libra stands in front of the TV. Aries takes the remote and turns off his screen, waiting for nonsense.*)

Libra: You tell the truth far more than necessary. (*Libra walks up to his husband, pissed off.*) I wish you'd lie more often; we'd be happier if you were a liar.

Aries: Why would you want me to lie more? (*Aries frowned, confused but not surprised.*) For a personified scale you seem obsessed with excess.

Libra: We aren't the happiest. (*Libra crosses his arms, defiant.*) We are good but not the happiest. We're not as happy as Aquarius and Leo, they're so glamorous together. (*Libra is staring his husband down. He's firm, as if he's found his footing on his husband's neck.*)

Aries: I love that they have my beloved Justice convinced of their joyless marriage. (*Aries is trying and failing not to laugh.*) Leo must be a front runner for an Emmy, Oscar or even Tony this year. Maybe he can EGOT! (*Aries succeeds in keeping his tone playful, barely hiding his growing irritation.*) Aquarius is quite the playwright, casting his poor husband in every secondary role.

Libra: Capricorn and Cancer are really sweet together. (*Libra persists. He's hoping his examples will crush a windpipe.*)

Aries: Cancer would rather be lived in than build a home with her wife. (*Aries is still the God of war. He is quite fine under pressure.*) She's a malignant brat asking her partner to make her into a project. Of course Capricorn is sweet to her. Only a self-absorbed psychiatrist would forgive such fuckery.

Libra: I like Sagittarius and Gemini together. Their love is star-crossed.

Aries: Every romance seems perfect if it is gay and starts with a sacreligious betrayal. (*He fights the urge to turn his show back on and looks Libra in the eye trying to muster a softness.*) I give it six months.

Libra: (*Uncrosses his arms and balls his hands to fists on his side, desperate.*) Scorpio—

Aries: Oh please, did you see them at Leo's dinner party? Social distancing like they don't shit in the same hole. You lose the second you go in with a love that has the gall to rot publically.

Libra: So what I get is nothing? (*Libra's voice wavers.*) I get no desperate measure. You call me Justice so easily and forget who you are. (*He's trying not to cry.*) Ruled by Mars and you won't even fight for me. I want war! I want certainty!

Aries: What war? (*Aries is a notorious hothead but his fire was recently put out. Love has found him and he's become a gasless stove.*) The war was won ages ago. Your dramatic ass is supposed to want peace. (*Maybe it is better said that he's become like a gasless stove. A fire is a fire.*) You're ruled by Venus. The patron of love begging for something he already has.

Libra: Then why don't I feel it from you? (*Libra's will to argue is fading.*) Shouldn't we feel bright and passionate? I want to be on fire!

Aries: Maybe give me some head then. Or call the siren, she's gotten real good with matches. (*In a conversation about what it is not, Aries can't pick between metaphor or the literal.*)

Libra: I want to feel like you want me. (*Libra wanted a hug and shopped for an argument instead.*) I want to feel like I'm not wasting my time.

Aries: You can't feel a concept. (*Aries is growing frustrated. Libra is good at igniting him.*) Here I am loving you and you're mad we aren't running for a finish line we already crossed. You're mad we aren't miserable because you've decided miserable is more interesting.

Libra: So if we aren't miserable what are we then? Tell me how you feel without mocking me? (*Libra decides to go for what he wants; a grand proclamation.*)

Aries: You want me to tell you how I love you? (*Aries is simmering down. Or attempting to.*) That's what you need from me right now?

Libra: Yes. (*He looks at his husband with a smile growing to the middle of his cheeks. Libra's defiance melting into sweetness.*)

Aries: Tomorrow we can do this all again and we can even do it the day after that. (*Aries is grinning, Libra is contagious.*) I'll love you enough to know you're just touch starved or bored. I'll never blame you though. (*Aries knows his husband, himself.*) We can blame it on full moons. Though, I know it's your retrograding planet's fault.

Libra: Venus is retrograding for three more weeks.

Aries: Eventually it'll go direct and I'll love you the whole time. (*Aries puts his hand out.*)

Libra: The whole time? (*Libra holds Aries hand and squeezes.*)

Aries: The whole time.

ELEMENT: AIR
The Siren knows it ends at sunset

DISCARD AT DAYBREAK

you decided this you said I'm sunset you said I'm sunrise I'm perfect to frame you I'd do anything to believe you you're darkness I'd endure anything to love you I knew you weren't asking permission I do as I'm told

I believe in love as service I wanted to set in all your seasons I'm not afraid of natural disaster I wanted to be hung up in the sky painted loved in whatever way you meant it I didn't know I'd be phased out that all I could hope for is that there'd be more than cracks when I crash I must affect you you know my bones are addicted to gravity I have to leave an impact

as I cave into the ground I hope you left a grave under the concrete I hope my casket is wrapped in cashmere but it won't matter you refuse to let me down gently I wasn't expecting to be thrown out I hope falling is a mindset that this only feels like dying but my wings have bones too I am not stronger than me

I want my love free falling in a different direction let it sink in the water I'll take drowning over crashing or you could just cut into me like you used to you were right that bleeding was the reason I'm gorgeous when day breaks my wounds are a part of the finale you need me for spectacle I'm a great opener I'm a great closer I'm supposed to survive when I rip across the sun I'm so pretty in pink

I won't close my eyes I don't want it to be over I throw my heart up out of my chest and before I hit the ground I hope you catch it I hope you pierce into it it keeps beating my love is incapable of dying it is always running red and you keep it in your hands knowing you never needed to hold to me to have me knowing I'd do anything to be an hour in your day

MUTABLE LOVERS
Former lovers are reduced to constellations, they died far from us

GEMINI

heaven is fog on the water
we are breaking up in flight
I feel every splinter love is
gravity you've decided
I'm someone worth losing

                                                VIRGO

                our time together thickens
                    the sky is fractured paint
            the air a soft blue I am great
                      at becoming I can't live
                    I stretch from the ground

SAGITTARIUS

hell is at capacity
and you are all I see
no one is making you
feel the way I am
I keep dreaming of fire

                                              PISCES

                    give the moon to space
              the rock melts over the horizon
            I'll still see you in the morning
        darkness is eventual and temporary
            I'll still see you in the morning
          Right? Tell me—I love you I love
                                you I love

PART TWO

The Inhabitants give the room its purpose. Your actions are stronger than any architect's intentions.

— Carmen Maria Machado

STATEMENTS IN THE FIRST HOUSE

Hi I'm a Cancer Rising and I'm addicted to my own sadness the reality show that'll lead to more honest confessions than this one I don't like making my bed because I heard on a bad sitcom that girls who are messy are better at sex but I'm always uncomfortable and I don't like to let anyone touch me still I'm hoping that every missing sock means a plethora of orgasms for whoever decides to love me before they realize I'm a yes man

and afraid of developing a concrete personality I've been told I'm detached but being detached is just the stage before I know exactly how to make sure you're never going to leave me I spent so long hating Virgo I let Capricorn ruin me in ways that led to Amy Dunne like exes specifically a Taurus that I can only talk about in mean tweets on my private Twitter account she wrote omegaverse fan fiction and said she'd slam dunk into my tits in a poem

I pretended to like so she'd never be angry at me and then she was angry with me anyways and I'll admit I only wrote that down because I imagine if she ever read that she would feel uncomfortable and invaded the way she made me feel the whole time she had me and I really only wrote that because I want to believe that I live in every ex's head the way they live in mine I'm a true communist they all occupy my mind rent free a true communist unless I'm looking for same day delivery and a pair jeans that can fit over my ass

anyways people aren't that obsessive especially air moons who discard when the object of their affection is no longer under their spell I keep trying to convince myself that my sexuality can be as loose as I am but every time someone touches me I feel like I'm burning and as you can see I've never been good at putting out fires but I won't know if I can love anyone unless

I love someone so much they don't scare me I like a good trial and error look at the homes I occupied I didn't mean for it to go down like this I love that dragon show I am traitor and lover of all gods the old and the new isn't there enlightenment through self destruction—fine—all twelve houses caved in on themselves because I can't tell the difference between trauma and desire and I'm so sorry but

I just want to believe that I can be vulnerable and versatile and I just want to be the best at everything I do but I can't even concentrate unless I take liquid meth or zone out for three hours a day and I don't know if when you asked for my name if you wanted to really know me or if you wanted to know what name to put on the case file I just spent so long hiding emotional truths I've become a punctured balloon and I promise I'll shut up soon all wounds heal at some point and if they don't I'm sure they'll pool and if not I'll faint before I finish bleeding out

SOUTH NODE
Meaning, the siren is good at this. Limerence as craft

Last night when I went to sleep I thought you'd die with the rest of it I'm not ashamed of my limerence love is malleable and if I have to love you to get through I can move past it

I would give you the moon but all I have is the sun and you're afraid to die in our fire

The last time I saw you I realized it was not enough to love you I can only hold so much space the universe is endless and I try to be but sadly I don't hold enough depth

All I have is the sun and it's too much for you to swallow

The last time I thought to love you I knew I couldn't be a final option endurance is admirable but I want to be squeezed out of a shell crack the mirror I can't keep reflecting back to you

I would give you the moon but all I have is the sun

At last I thought to save myself I thought an ending is better on a cliff I hit the earth to know there is nothing left to know there is no love just because I am giving it

I would give you the moon I would give you the moon I would give you the moon

ELEMENT: AIR
The siren grows wings and forgets themself

THE SIREN IS AIR SURFING

I'm not worried about you dying
but I can save you tonight
don't be moody I can end in heaven
hell is almost at capacity
only one spot left the choice
obvious between fawning

siren or love bombing vampire
you should've released your demons
you can still get on your knees fucking
is a type of exorcism maybe we could've been
happier adventurous no it's too late
for reimaginings

your soul is in your mouth I would let you
tongue it in me but I'm not a home
you can return to our house
is splintered on the water
and in the age of Aquarius the tornado
takes me to Eden

the witch is dead she nearly killed me
I didn't tell her my body is holy
water poor thing but her broom
has a full tank you can ride it
with me or end at a ten story drop
dear god put misery

on another bitch's soundtrack
our love can't be a horror movie
leaving doesn't have to kill you
if the air is dark enough you can survive
we only have a few hours to sunrise
scatter the air if you must
we will be breaking

up in flight

THE ACQUISITION OF THE SECOND HOUSE

This is going to hurt isn't it crazy I
never thought I'd feel like this stop stand
over there do not move closer I am not
in the mood for softness choose me
choose me at a distance I prefer clues

over declarations there is no romance in
statements I don't want a contract it
all ends with I love you doesn't it I don't
want it to end what is there to look
forward to after you say it hold my hand

quietly kiss me softly let the room melt
to silence we don't have to discuss it
I'm not in the mood to know anything
I don't stand tall in your arms I don't
stand at all you can't listen you're stronger

than my defenses you pull closer my head
was made for the crook of your neck
chose me chose me clarity is a warning
you cease all anxiety my defeat
is the paced beat in your chest

my defeat is in the calm of my breath
it's over isn't it pretending
I could love at a distance
pretending I could love
anyway anywhere anyone but you

SYNASTRY: OPPOSITION
Picture, love as an island about to drown

THEIR MOON IS IN ARIES

when you lay next to me my name is love honey or please not right now and I identify with all of them

if love is possible I want it far away from me

you are only interested in my feelings if you can't see them and I mean it is possible to bench yourself and lose anyway

if I'm in love we were fucked before we even started

at some point the houses must be the problem I brought you to the island to save us so how is it that I can feel the ocean itching to drown us out

if love is meant to thrive here I'm mad that I need you

I would give you the moon and I don't know if that means I'm in love or if I wanna be a god and let the waves have you ahead of schedule

if love is your name it isn't familiar to me

this would be easier if I didn't view softness as a threat I am scared of you for all the reasons I want you around

if love is rational it wants to keep running from me

when I give you the moon and our island starts flooding and the moon cracks I'll say it—

if love dies at the edge of this island I'll bury your head in the sand

THIRD HOUSE MIND PALACE

the ability to remember
depends on how you view language
is it a space or a promise
when you talk I see teeth
falling out of your mouth
I am a master of dream

interpretation in all of mine
you are running you speak like a door
I am passing through
I should not attempt to follow
I know the hallway leads
to door to door an endless
vacation I am busy I do not

have time I am speaking
to build a shelf
for a room I spoke
into existence all my words are
layered with subtext I want
a foundation I want a home

I sing and all the faucets
pierce the porcelain with memory
you lie and you lose
all sharpness I cannot
be lied to I built a home
in conversation language is a space

before it is a way to say—
you are leaving
do you know the hallway
is not endless
if you turn back
turn back

FOURTH HOUSE INVENTORY

It's been a year since
the house collapsed but
I am still looking through
the carnage I'm missing

the pair of socks laying
under the bed I'm looking
for our vases shattered over
the carpet our names engraved
on the side of the bed frame

tell me you never loved me that
I won't find you here say that
I won't find dead flower petals
love letters that the promises

we broke compressed into graves
I want to stop revisiting
the site I want to feel
comfortable in my new space
I still feel the way I did that night

floating up passed the ceiling
could you tell me I am not
the only ghost haunting
the space our comforter survived

this ending if I curled up
into it would you still be next to me
your hands wrapped around
my neck would you tell me how to leave
without feeling like I lost myself here

SYNASTRY: SQUARE
Picture, love as dreaming awake

TO YOU FOR ME

Sometimes when you say I love you I
think you say it just to say it to someone/like when you call me
honey it's because she isn't there/I'm a placeholder/close enough
to someone who loves you the way you expect to be loved/but
I picture our lives in beaches and cloudless skies/ you can really
only appreciate blue skies without dust/and you call me honey
and I wonder if you only mean me when you say it

I hate sleeping with other people

I tell that lie every time I talk to
cuddlers and touch starved people/just so they know not to get too
close/so I can curl in on myself and feel like I am enough to fill the
holes in me/maybe there are no holes and I'm just softer in some
places/and if I squish myself enough I will feel hard/I will feel full/I
am enough for me—

You knew this and we slept together
anyway

Not like how lovers sleep together/
we aren't lovers/although I love you/you're on the cusp of loving
me I can feel it but I don't trust it/I can't trust you never ever—*I'm
lying I do*/Our feet are touching under the covers/I'm tempted
to pull away/I don't really want to/ You keep saying you're cold/
I think this means you want me to be closer/ I don't take it like
that I just ask what you need/ you don't say anything—

We talk about buying an island
with cool blue waters and warm yellow suns/I wonder when you

picture it if you see her there too/then the image is cracked because I only ever see the both of us/but there is no both us there's the idea/ then there's me and you/then there's you her—

I like the corner of the bed that
touches the wall

We sleep facing each other but we
aren't really/we're just staring at each other/you tell me you love me/the first thing I want to do is doubt you and I do/then you say of course because you do (*it's just not enough*)/you ask me three times if I love you and I can't think of a reason you would need reassurance/here I am not yours and completely yours/I think maybe you just want to hear I'm in love with you/but I refuse to say it to someone who can't say it too—

Our home on the island is made of
glass and palm trees/we keep cover when it rains so it's like we live inside the island instead of on top of it/I wish we could sink ourselves in it to forget the idea of a place where things don't belong to us/you don't just belong to me—

We sleep back to back still touching
I hate sleeping with other people/because I am enough for me/but you're so warm and I'm a little drunk—

I can see our feet in warm sands/
curling our toes as waves hit the shore/creating cold sands that stick on us/I think how happy we could be/how happy I am next to you—

I fall fast asleep knowing that I am
mine you belong to someone else and

you don't want me but you love me
anyway

ELEMENT: EARTH
The Siren grows legs and loses themself

THIS SIREN IS SPRINTING

I want to sing you
a love song
I want the solo
handed to me

a heavy dilemma
the chorus sung by sea witches
who've stolen my voice
they love you

they resent me
I don't know what it means
to love you
I want a fantasy

I want magic
I want rose coloured visions
when I picture us
I see many faces

none of them mine
I know you well too well
and you are running
from something

the song I want
to sing is not written for me
the theft
was always my doing—

I've been running from
something and you won't
run with me try
run to me

FIFTH HOUSE THEATRE

all antagonists deserve
a happy ending I hear
the monologues
and I agree with them

a movie is only good
if it's fighting against
itself I refuse to tear
up the house it belongs

to me in a Rachel Berry
Renaissance the parade
rains acid water I know
you are so very mad at me

I know I could've left you
gently but the fifth house
is for glamour and fire
the sun sets our bedroom

aflame and it wouldn't
matter anyway a boundary
is a stake in the heart to
an energy vampire and you

can't get close to me
daylight is doing
as promised
the wicked witch was my ass

the whole time I've put a curse
on us and I'm the bad guy
if I never loved you
I'm the bad guy

but as the credits run
over our story our end meets
a standing ovation

PROPAGATING THE SIXTH HOUSE

I am into the rise of myself I'll be a botanical empire the separation between my body and soul are closing I used to leave space for all to grow flower toxins and fruits but I loved weeds the most

rose colours are just the name of the ivy I let invade my walls I would make my old wounds new because they itch when they start to heal if the pain had to exist

I wanted it unbearable I couldn't let it scar I was against memories I couldn't feel my skin is soil if I want the hurt to stay alive I'll give it roots I'll dig my head in the water

no one propagates trauma like me I am the green thumb everything I grow thrives if I want it to and when I decided to kill my love for you the space begun to flower

I felt my heart through the walls no one told me my body was this powerful all the things my mind could do that I've been a garden witch the whole time

my air purifying tropical magic like the viper I still grow in the dark I can go a long time without water but the prophecy warned I've been afraid of flight I'll surrender to it

and you will watch what happens when I nurture the home I'm in I cut the weed at roots and violets sprout I am the garden so let me show you what's possible when I stretch

from the ground

SYNASTRY: INCONJUNCT
Picture, love as childhood memory

THE SUN WAS IN PISCES

my mom hates the colour red the rules of her occult tell her it's an evil colour when it sits around my eyes she resents it the tears that follow she resents them she wonders when I became an ocean I want to know when hers ran dry I see its remnants at the corner of her iris the red has faded now rose coloured she is love in my image I learned to love everyone like her

if I'm not running there's no way to keep my feet on the ground

this morning on my way to work I notice the hoarder's house has been cleaned up the garbage covering a garden with a Buddha at its centre flowers are blooming it is beautiful I miss all the mess that hid it

if tripping over us was an option my head would've already run red into the pavement

my boss tells me it's important to take time off he says I might see things I don't like I'm wondering if I'll ever meet me when it happened I'm wondering if I'll recognize my wounds in someone else and then he tells me we are not in the business of saving anyone

if drowning was possible I wouldn't have ran in the first place

I wish my mom knew that red meant passion that passion is powerful she once told me if she felt everything that ever happened to her she wouldn't know how to function that she wouldn't know how to speak her words go over my head I wish she knew a voice exists after cracking open that it only burns because living requires setting fires to feel warmth

I know better than to say I was running from me I was always running to her I am always running to her but the finish line is not in her direction

MIDHEAVEN
Meaning, the siren understands their world.
They would still see it burning

America does not know me
yet I dream of her it's promised
I'll meet her in San Junipero
Our happy ending in the afterlife
I am in love with dreams I can't sleep with
the moor of my life dreams I'll come home to her in a funeral
car she'll be dressed in white

The night of my death is the day
before our wedding
Till then she is promised to someone else
She falls in union with Uncle Sam
and believes it to be love

America is a comphet dyke
she can't tell the difference
between passion and a house that is burning
She wears a *straight is great* t-shirt
All the queers who love her don't believe
it's unrequited America is to an outsider
as the moon is to a poet

I am under her influence
We are speaking past each other
I am a river bottled in flesh my proximity to her
decides when I am drowning

But I can be oh so American I don't see
the difference between patriotism
and houses that are burning
America I've become a danger to myself

I want the comfort of arms
I want you suffocate me from the inside out

How long will you pretend
that he will hold up a flag in his likeness
offer your hostages a release
you hope your love will surrender
on one knee returning your hand

I imagine it'll lead you back to me
But your tides are free
I want to believe you're a damsel but
the martyr died the day
you got your name

America is a comphet dyke
she can't tell the difference
between loving me
and awaiting my burial

If you can wear a pride flag
to the next bombing
Collateral and equality
are synonymous

America is a comphet dyke she can no longer
tell the difference between guilt and spite
She believes she's immortal she's forgotten
she is coming home to me and I've been
oh so American I've never seen the difference
between bloodshed and freedom

America's gotten colder
in her self awareness no longer in chains
she resents her roots
She can't tell the difference
between love and massacre

I will not mince my words for a country
entitled and blameless
I need white men sorry to me

I want God the Pope
I want the mailman to be sorry to me
And I'm a rockstar poet
I am ruled by the moon
this is my Nicki Minaj phase
I'll let it triangulate

Canada is like a soundproof room
He believes peacekeeping is a gun's silencer
We are all liberal
You may like it here
If you're into bright smiles and colourful
parades while Indigenous women go missing

All birthday parties take place over mass graves
our anthem sung proudly in the key of apathy
He is oh so nice all executions end in apologies
Canada takes after his mother and
Britain's grown distasteful of his sibling

No tact

America has done everything
but gaslight her lovers into delusion
Now the entire west is oh so American
we can no longer see the difference
between whiteness and an automatic weapon
history is cyclical

I watch the same wound open and close
like a pierced artery America
views scars as the end of a conversation
Canada as proof that nothing
is currently happening but a wound can only
open so much before it infects

America is a comphet dyke
She can't tell the difference
between disobedience and a rebellion

I can't promise that I will be faithful
when I come home to her
if America can only hold me when I'm dying
but I don't want her to forget

America I know that I belong to you
A songstress likened my body to fruit
And a poet begged for a song
A city of ash our house covered in smoke

You are a series of mythologies
An antagonist built by stolen people
from a thousand ships
You're an empire built on land
of the people you were stolen from

America is a comphet dyke
She can no longer tell the difference
between a hero and a villain
And I am oh so Canadian
I cannot love you
until our house is burning

SLOW DANCE IN THE SEVENTH HOUSE

I'll love anyone who wants to dance with me in any room in any place
in our kitchen

right before dinner or when there is nothing but coke

in the fridge maybe I never gave anyone the chance to want to
but I used to think love was a girl

who had a giant pantry in her house I never had any snacks
in mine so I ended up thinking love was just abundance

in something I'm lacking I thought forever was a reflection of wants
myself in the body

of a person I wouldn't mind fucking but then I considered love as more
as saying I'm sorry

because union is saying *I feel* instead of *I need* it is two people
promising stability

vows as infographics but I had no desire to fall in love with good
communication love became

dancing taking me by the hand because I want to be taken
love is not absence

it is would you like to followed by no I'd love to

EIGHTH HOUSE MIRACLE

tonight I believe in miracles I will
not bear witness to our devastation
do not ruin us with the truth
if you want to be candid lie

to me bluntly tonight I believe
in God i believe that delusion
is a virtue I am pure
in my missteps if you didn't

mean to mislead me I didn't
mean to crack the house
there is no end if we never start I
don't tell you what it means to love

you stop looking at me like the sun sets
in my eyes this is how we stay together
we stay crystallized here the flame
between us does not burn us out

tonight when I say I love you
I mean it sans prayer for more
our home stays intact
the moon falls over us

SYNASTRY: TRINE
Picture, love as acceptance of history

TO ME FOR YOU

this is going to be painful
days at the beach watching
the sky bruised boats
sink with passengers

I remember thinking it was
so far away islands framing
bleeding skies and freezing water
I remember her the way

water filled my lungs
suffocating before I even dipped
my feet in now you're next
to me the sky's the clearest

it's ever been no dust only blue
and the sun shaped like the moon
against the water where I wait
for our time to end

I wait for a hurricane to hit
the shore and drown us
I wait to live to say I told you
so instead you lean your head

on my shoulder say something
about how beautiful
it is and as it falls to night
I lean on you too

ELEMENT: FIRE
The Siren adapts to fire and gains enlightenment

THAT SIREN IS SETTING FIRES

light me on fire I promise
I won't make a sound
you need a match for a starter
the truth is gasoline

let me pour it out no one
is making you feel the way I am
making you feel you don't
love anyone the way you could

love me as if we are playing target
practice put a lighter to all arrows
set the little fires slow burning
is a sure way to start forever

and I want that with you
go ahead light us a fire
go ahead use me for warmth
go ahead you won't burn alone

NINTH HOUSE STELLIUM
after and with blake levario

1. siren migration

I did my best I searched for   nothing but ruin   I learn to love myself
enlightenment through self   destruction i binge houses   as a full thing i retrace
destruction i found water   and fire i come back alive   my disappearing footsteps
i found warmth and lost me   i find myself in new oceans   it's been nice to know you

       I searched for   nothing but ruin
                                    I binge houses   I retrace
destruction I found water   and fire
               and lost me   I find myself   to know you

I did my best   I learn   love

                                                                 to know you

2. rodeo clowns

when the gates release
away—suspend belief
like when you left home
you ended up at the rodeo
to hurt me—but I want you

out comes the danger
you could be something else
all of your fuck-ups neon
looking bulls in the eye
to *not* hurt me

and you're so used to running
you could be filling up new space
visible for miles and miles
saying, I know you're not *trying*
okay?

3. a new space

when I learn to love myself
in new oceans
I retrace your footsteps
you're so used to running

I come back alive
visible for miles and miles
I love myself
we are filling new space

I found warmth
it's nice knowing you
as a full thing
we found water

I found warmth

retrace our footsteps   love   in   new space

DELIVERANCE FROM THE TENTH HOUSE

dear god I was looking for a solution
but I've learned a house that exists on bones only haunts
I know you did not expect a celebration in your absence
but I couldn't help it you died I started the applause
you thought to deliver me from evil and I sank into it

I found what loves me under water
I became light on the dark side of the moon
you thought chaos would lead me to heaven
I saw your wrath and ran from it no god I don't do love by myself
no I became a ghost and hoped it'd lead me to you

but those who love me brought me back to life
and those who love me don't ask when you'll save me
all my dreams of paradise are the hell you described
and all my dreams come true
no I can no longer beg you to love me

if I don't know what it is to love you no I am done begging to love
no the apocalypse is all or nothing thinking isn't that something
I find love in the house but I don't wish to rebuild it
if I have to save you for the house to stand then I'll leave it in ashes
I can't sacrifice myself there is no authority if what's left is worship

If I have to worship to love than I'd rather be loveless
but no the rapture doesn't find me looking for a saviour no
I won't be on my knees when I pray you don't answer
the kingdom was made with bloodied hands
I won't be saved in isolation not if I have to be swallowed by sky

to go to heaven I'd rather die under water
no deliver me from obligation no deliver me into freedom no
deliver me into a love that isn't Holy dear god
I learned to love and no you don't do it no I learned to love
and no I do it I didn't find love in the kingdom you left for me

no I know you don't love me because I found it
no I know love because of me I keep the tenth house
in ruins I let your demons haunt the space
and when I invite them to dinner I sit at the head
of a table of ashes and when we start our feast I know we'll end full

SYNASTRY: SEXTILE
Picture, love with a fatalist school of thought

THE ISLAND ROSE IN CANCER

this world is not ending the comet
is a pebble skipping on water
and even if it was I'd give it all up

for you oh honey time is inescapable
there is no way out of us
relax I'm not pulling you

from the water but I'll sit next
to you please don't drown
this island is unlivable

without you just look at this view
the sun setting into the ocean
smoke filling the air breathe it in

fire is unavoidable the water is shallow
don't dig your head in dip your feet
sit with it you belong next to me
I don't want anyone else next to me

THE BASEMENT IN THE ELEVENTH HOUSE
for Amyrah Uddin

I did not know love before I knew you isn't that something
where do I think of us first I think of large fields deer running
at dusk an inability to run after them classrooms in the middle
of playgrounds

where do you think of us second remember your room in the
basement Bailey and I cut magazine papers to decorate our
apartment and I thought of your walls papered in *Vogue* a best
friend is a tricky thing when your home caves the second you're
born into it

I tried to find home in people but Warsan said they are not
meant to be lived in we don't allow that you love me right next
to me you forgive me I forgive you we blame our fathers we
blame our mothers we blame everyone for everything it's all
their fault I'm a terrible gossip we are so perfect everyone thinks
so I asked everyone in the world

you are flawless and I feel perfect next to you where do I picture us first in my basement where mom bought thirty packs
of Halloween chips for your birthday we are always watching
something *Maury* at yours *Warm Bodies* at mine *Modern Family*
at yours *Glee* at mine our friendship starts below the foundation
we miss the tornado that caves the house the basement is safe

and we're having too much fun down there I am laughing too
loud we don't hear the house rip our jokes save us from disaster
we are unfazed walking past the rubble your mom gave us five
good dollars we want to spend it on something useful and after
the pizza run

we come back the house fully standing can you believe it how it rose from underground can you believe we saved the house can you believe it's because you love me and I love you

look at it from the ground up it's bigger it's better than before I love the dining table I love the living room I love the porch I love your home thank you for having me lets sun bathe before we go inside I am only here for a little while but it's so nice to see you it's been forever how have you been what do you want to watch tonight

INVENTING THE TWELFTH HOUSE

Tonight I will rewrite
music I will unfurl
a feeling out

of an old one
I'm like any sea witch
I sing lullabies

to bring you to sleep
a long one I know my love
is a devastation

I pray I can be
the villain I am
scared of all

I'm becoming tired
and less patient
wounded irate

and certain
a siren accustomed
to water I knew

what would become
of this Island that
loving you like

this is a fear
of the self I don't know
who I am or how

anyone could know
me I create a home
to prove no one

can survive it—you're
drowning you do
as the moon

does a pirate you
control the tides in hopes
they'll save you

but you are tethered
above the water—this is my home
and this ocean holds memory

I don't want to pretend
I know loving you
does bite down

and you wonder
why they all leave you
my blood is holy

water I was not meant
to cut open—there is no escape
your feet are so heavy

on the ground you were
wrong to see a body of water as
romance tides as limerence

me as an anchor—the love
of your life has a rope
around their neck

stop tugging
I don't want to choke

ELEMENT: WATER
The Siren discovers love and rest

THESE SIRENS ARE SWIMMING

I don't believe in love
at first sight but I can
know I will love someone
the second I see them
the key is the word yet

we are covered in blue
an illusion of clarity
you cannot hold water
in your hands it runs through
it runs clear it remembers

before it washes us clean
it holds before it fills
our lungs and I
have done everything
to not sit in it

I tried to grow legs
and run from us
I tried to let the fire
burn us slowly

but this was always
the solution to forget
the sky and all its colour
to lay my head underwater

to hit the sand I knew it
when I saw you I saw it
I kept seeing you visions
took over my dreams

it's okay lay your head
next to mine darling
we were never capable
of drowning

SYNASTRY: CONJUNCT
Picture, love as is

SUN SONG

I remember the island and when I became it
when I was a full realized thing when I was salt
water when I flowed to dehydrate to end
the idea of love as a series of breaking points
the sun is now only invested in ruining dull skin
it's fallen in love with me I remember when I lost interest
I tried to say everything I hadn't felt in months I like to
fall out of love the way I'm supposed to fall in it in
grand proclamations I like to leave screaming
I am bad at tense when I told you I loved you
I should've said it like that I should've said loved
and I want this to be about us I want this feeling
to belong to you I am not in love with memory
I've talked myself off the edge I am fully present
there is no quick sand to sink into you are long gone
the you isn't you here—I want this to be a bad thing
thank you for making it easy it is difficult in the way it isn't at all
I am not isolated the words don't come out but I'm no longer
afraid of choking I just can't let you fall out from the sky
the water is drinkable but I am only good at drowning
yet the waves never catch me my feet never leave the sand
this ocean is not as deep as it should be I can't get lost in anything
when I look up there is nothing sinking me I'm addicted to breathing
I can feel the sun warm on my skin the sky splitting into sunset though
it never bleeds and it never breaks I am never startled I am not afraid
of your absence this is not a confession when the sun leaves
to give the moon to space I know I'll see you in the morning this is
not painful the horizon melts over me because it has to because
darkness is eventual and temporary I can say what I mean because
I mean it—I love you I love
you I love

NORTH NODE
Meaning, understanding is not practice.
Letting go is a pull of the door

the trauma I was holding I put it down I can't
let sadness be a virtue and wasn't it didn't it
lead me here a life of breathlessness and bruising
I think there is much to learn from water

how it empties how my home survived a dense
emptiness I can't live here the foundation doesn't shake
my house adapts to the violence but I can't love
the siren must swim away from the house

there are people who love me out there
and I remember where I come from this island
a series of pains and triumphs I've survived many wars
holding my breath in the name of love a falsehood there is

no love in self violence don't mind the feeling I found
a home in sinking it took care of me there are memories
in the waves warmth colouring the water before dark I called it
home for a reason but above water I feel safe that can house me too

ACKNOWLEDGEMENTS

First and foremost I would like to thank Jim Johnstone for giving me the opportunity to not only publish my first book but my first chapbook. I am forever indebted to you for publishing my work and for trusting it and believing it. Kirby for publishing my first and second chapbooks which feature one of the first versions of the seventh house poem. Lastly, Daniel Tysdal for making me the writer I am today, a writer who feels sure and strong in my own voice because of my time as your student.

I would also like to thank all the publications that have published the house poems: *Pigeon Pages* (special shout out to Peach on your edits for Inventing The Twelfth House!!), *OOMPH press*, *Ampersand Review*, *The Shore*, *HAD* and a special shout out to *Block Party Mag* and Isla McLaughlin and Joseph Donato— Ryanne and I talked many times about starting a literary mag in undergrad and I think we won't now because this will definitely be the best and my most favourite mag to come out of UTSC.

I would like to shout out the Sagittarius I stopped knowing in 2018. The misery you caused me soft launched my career so I'm gonna say we even and also thanks!!

I would like to thank my loves who occupy the eleventh house: Ryanne, Sarah, Camryn, Nayana, Janat, Alanna, Zina, Urbana, Jessica, Hannah, Lucie, Cas, Cai, Noor, Em, Sanna, Téa and of course Amyrah who the last eleventh house poem is dedicated too. Thank you all for showing me the different ways friendship can save you and all the different ways love can help you rebuild yourself after disaster. I love you all so much and I'm grateful for you.

My loves in the fourth house: Bailey, Ally and Adina thank you for showing me that a physical home can be a safe place for all the ways you held me, for making being a homebody more fun and lively than I ever thought it could be, for supporting me for all the ways we have held each other. I love you so much.

Lastly, I would like to thank Blake for listening to me complain about motifs and calling me corny at the end of a thirty minute rant about motifs, for despite that response to my thirty minute rant taking a month to go over my book, your edits and for creating the form that suits my ninth house stellium perfectly and writing it with me. For occupying the ninth house and for being there when we can only rely on each other. Thank you, I'll always be grateful for that.

Victoria Mbabazi is a Pisces with an Aries Moon. Their first chapbook *chapbook* is available with Anstruther Press and their double chapbook *Flip* is available with Knife | Fork | Book. This is their first full-length poetry collection. They live in Brooklyn, New York.